AN IDEAS INTO ACTION GUIDEBOOK

Accountability
Taking Ownership of Your Responsibility

IDEAS INTO ACTION GUIDEBOOKS

Aimed at managers and executives who are concerned with their own and others' development, each guidebook in this series gives specific advice on how to complete a developmental task or solve a leadership problem.

LEAD CONTRIBUTOR	Henry Browning
CONTRIBUTORS	Greg Laskow
	Jennifer Martineau
	Jim Shields
	Richard Walsh

DIRECTOR OF ASSESSMENTS, TOOLS, AND PUBLICATIONS	Sylvester Taylor
MANAGER, PUBLICATION DEVELOPMENT	Peter Scisco
EDITOR	Stephen Rush
EDITOR	Karen Lewis
DESIGN AND LAYOUT	Joanne Ferguson
COVER DESIGN	Laura J. Gibson
	Chris Wilson, 29 & Company

CCL No. 451
ISBN No. 978-1-60491-116-9

CENTER FOR CREATIVE LEADERSHIP
POST OFFICE BOX 26300
GREENSBORO, NORTH CAROLINA 27438-6300
336-288-7210
WWW.CCL.ORG/PUBLICATIONS

AN IDEAS INTO ACTION GUIDEBOOK

Accountability
Taking Ownership of Your Responsibility

Henry Browning

Center for
Creative
Leadership

www.ccl.org

THE IDEAS INTO ACTION GUIDEBOOK SERIES

This series of guidebooks draws on the practical knowledge that the Center for Creative Leadership (CCL®) has generated, since its inception in 1970, through its research and educational activity conducted in partnership with hundreds of thousands of managers and executives. Much of this knowledge is shared—in a way that is distinct from the typical university department, professional association, or consultancy. CCL is not simply a collection of individual experts, although the individual credentials of its staff are impressive; rather it is a community, with its members holding certain principles in common and working together to understand and generate practical responses to today's leadership and organizational challenges.

The purpose of the series is to provide managers with specific advice on how to complete a developmental task or solve a leadership challenge. In doing that, the series carries out CCL's mission to advance the understanding, practice, and development of leadership for the benefit of society worldwide. We think you will find the Ideas Into Action Guidebooks an important addition to your leadership toolkit.

Table of Contents

EXECUTIVE BRIEF

More and more organizations are putting in a lot of effort to measure engagement and foster empowerment in order to develop a culture of accountability—taking ownership of projects, processes, and problems that cut across lines of position and formal responsibility. Whereas responsibility is generally delegated by the boss, the organization, or by virtue of position, accountability is having a sense of ownership for the task and the willingness to face the consequences that come with success or failure. The challenge with accountability is that it is intrinsic: it depends entirely on the individual's—or, in some cases, the team's—choice to act with greater accountability. There are three levels of commitment that organizations seek from their employees: engagement, empowerment, and, ultimately, accountability. Through this guidebook you will learn how your organization and its leaders can create a culture that fosters accountability by focusing on five areas: *support, freedom, information, resources,* and *goal and role clarity.* You will also be able to evaluate individual leaders in your organization in terms of how well they exhibit accountable behaviors and traits. Finally, you will see how to turn around the factor that is the biggest obstacle to accountability—fear in the workplace—and turn it into trust.

Being Accountable

Organizations committed to developing their talent are constantly striving to push their managers to accept greater levels of responsibility. Official responsibility often comes from holding a particular position, but more and more managerial challenges require leaders to take initiative without having full authority for the process or the outcomes—in other words, to be accountable. Organizations spend a great deal of energy measuring engagement and fostering empowerment to develop a culture of accountability. These efforts are all designed to develop people so they can make sound decisions and be willing to stand behind those decisions. Organizations want people to take ownership of projects, processes, and problems that cut across lines of position and formal responsibility. In short, they are asking for higher levels of personal accountability from their employees.

But accountability is often difficult to define for organizations and even more difficult to articulate to those being developed within a talent pipeline. This guidebook is designed to provide a language and practical tools for developing norms and a culture of accountability in your team, group, or organization.

For the purposes of this guidebook, it is important that some distinctions be made between the terms *accountability* and *responsibility*. Often the literature uses these words interchangeably. For this particular model the following distinction will be made:

A person may be delegated the *responsibility* for a task by the boss, the organization, or by virtue of position. *Accountability*, however, refers to an acknowledgement and internalization of a sense of ownership for a task and the willingness to face the consequences that come with success or failure.

In leadership roles, accountability is the acknowledgment and assumption of responsibility for actions, products, decisions, and policies, including administration, governance, and implementation within the scope of the role or employment position and encompassing the obligation to report, explain, and be answerable for resulting consequences.

The challenge with accountability is that it is intrinsic, just like engagement and empowerment. An environment or culture that promotes accountability can be fostered, but the end result is totally dependent on the individual's—or sometimes, as we will see later in this guidebook, the team's—choice to act with greater accountability.

Much of the accountability literature attempts to make a distinction between people who act with great accountability and people who act as victims of circumstances and who are not willing to own the outcomes and ultimately the consequences of failed actions. The issue, however, may be less about *victims* and *accountable people* and more about creating the correct structures, systems, and support that will foster a culture of accountability—conditions that encourage people to fully own their decisions.

To be sure, most people seem to be more than willing to own success. But that is the crux of the problem: people will attempt to attach themselves to success, but if they are not just as willing to own their mistakes, organizational performance and learning will come to a standstill. Organizations will argue that their accountability issues arise only when people are unwilling to take ownership of failure.

Levels of Commitment

The first thing to understand about the feelings and beliefs concerning accountability is that they are intrinsic in nature. In other words, we can create the conditions to maximize feelings and beliefs of accountability in others, but for the link to work those others must have a sense of accountability within themselves.

To understand accountability in organizations it is best to describe the different levels of individual commitment that organizations try to get from their employees. The literature points out and defines three distinct stages that employees go through—*engagement, empowerment,* and *accountability.*

Organizations define the *engaged* employee as one who is fully involved in and enthusiastic about his or her work and who thus will act in a way that furthers the organization's interests. In basic psychological terms, it is engagement at the cognitive level (head), the emotional level (heart), and the behavioral level (hands or feet—the *doing*). To achieve this type of engagement, individuals usually need to know that what they do contributes to important work and that they have some freedom to apply their natural intellect to achieve positive outcomes. They also need to see that the tasks they do and the actions they take are aligned with the organization's mission, vision, strategy, and goals.

Empowered employees make their own decisions with regard to their tasks. Once employees are engaged and their actions are aligned with the organization's interests, enhancing their decision-making abilities coupled with confidence-building opportunities lead to empowerment. Nowadays, more and more managers are practicing the concept of empowerment of their subordinates to provide them with more and better opportunities to take charge and make decisions. But even with empowerment, employees sometimes seek protection behind the authority of the supervisor.

Empowerment is a developmental transition that many organizations fail to recognize. Organizations need to develop their employees in a way that allows them to slowly but surely take on increasingly complex decisions. Without the safety net of the boss and the organization, however, many employees are afraid to do so.

Empowerment, like engagement, is intrinsic in nature. Organizations can create the conditions for empowerment but they cannot guarantee that employees will take on greater responsibility. To create an environment that fosters greater empowerment, leaders need to provide

- confidence—communicating respect for the individual's skills and abilities
- communication—transparency combined with frequency
- clear boundaries—formed by measurements, protocol, and authority
- support—not micromanaging but trusting
- recognition—of initiative and responsible risk taking

Here are some helpful hints for managers who seek to empower the people they lead.

- Tell employees clearly what you need from them. Let them know the areas in which they are free to make decisions.
- Develop their decision-making skills and create a learning environment.
- Set achievable goals.
- Provide them with all the information they need to make decisions.
- Encourage them to share their thoughts and doubts among themselves and with management.

With *accountability*, we must consider a much deeper relationship between the employee and the work—one that transcends the trappings of responsibility that come with position. The employee who is accountable will make decisions and own the consequences of those decisions regardless of whether the results turn out to be positive or negative.

Inspiring accountability in the workplace requires a two-pronged approach.

- First, leaders need to secure ever-greater levels of commitment to the work, the business, the strategy, and ultimately the organization.

- Second, they need to remove unnecessary fear from the decision-making culture—the kind of fear that prevents people from acknowledging their mistakes.

You can use the scorecard on the following pages to rate how well your organization and its leaders create a culture that encourages accountability.

Focus Areas

CCL's research has yielded a simple model that is designed to build a culture of accountability (see Figure 1, page 13). The five focus areas are

- support—organizational, supervisory, and work team support

- freedom—the freedom to direct important aspects of the work

- information—access to relevant information needed to do the work

- resources—access to enough resources to do the work

- goal and role clarity—clarity of the goal, responsibility, and consequences of action or inaction

Accountability Scorecard

Rate how well you think your organization and its leaders employ these practices of accountability. The scale ranges from 1 (not very descriptive of us) to 5 (very descriptive of us).

____ 1. We are specific and clear about roles, team leadership, and individual ownership in a way that eases confusion.

____ 2. People have a sense of ownership for the results of their team.

____ 3. We face squarely what went right and what did not, and why.

____ 4. When things don't go right, we don't hear denial, blaming, excuses, and scapegoating.

____ 5. The team leader is held accountable for the results of the team, even when results fall short of rising expectations.

____ 6. The accounting aims at improvement, not punishment.

____ 7. People expect that their actions, decisions, and behaviors will be evaluated.

____ 8. Leaders take the initiative to claim and create what they need to succeed.

____ 9. People are held accountable if they don't do what they say they will do.

____ 10. When facing competing priorities (for example, cutting costs versus improving customer service), people feel that they have the freedom, support, and control to decide how to navigate the conflict.

____ 11. People feel and can see a strong link between what they do and overall team performance.

If your total score is less than 33, your organization and its leaders probably need to take a look at how they can better create a culture that encourages accountability.

Of the above eleven items, which two have improved most in the past eighteen months?

Which two might you be overdoing?

Which two would benefit you most to improve in the next eighteen months?

In addition, leaders have to balance between two competing considerations: process and results. Indicate below how well your leaders balance these two considerations, with 1 indicating that they put too much weight on the process, 3 indicating that the balance is just right, and 5 indicating that they put too much weight on results.

____ a. Leaders are held accountable for the standards and procedures they use to make decisions.

____ b. Leaders are held accountable for the outcomes of their decisions.

Figure 1. The Five Components of Building Accountability

13

Support

In complex organizations, support for major projects can be both broad and deep. In general terms, there are three types of support that are most crucial for fostering accountability. The first is an organizational level of support. The second centers around the role of the supervisor or boss. The third is the human resources assigned to the task—the manager's team.

Support for accountability has a structural aspect as well as a cultural aspect.

The structural component comprises systems that provide goal and role clarity, that grant authority and official power, that supply information from internal and market sources, and that furnish resources for operational implementation. Following are some questions you can ask to determine the degree of structural support for accountability at each of the three levels.

- Organizational level
  - Does the organization publicly acknowledge the importance of the work and the people doing it?
  - Do our strategy and tactics align with the work's mission and vision?
  - Are there clear processes to benchmark our progress?

- Supervisory level
  - Does my boss acknowledge the importance of my work?
  - Does my boss provide me with clear authority to make decisions and direct the work?
  - Does my boss take an active role in coaching me through my own thinking and logic processes?

- Team level
  - Does the team believe in the importance of the work?
  - Have I been able to hire the right talent to accomplish the work?
  - Do I have access to extended technical resources to augment the team's skill set?

     – Do I have the authority to eliminate or develop poor
       performers?
     – Does the team have clear guidelines regarding decisions
       they should make and decisions they should defer to a
       higher authority?

Figure 2. What Kind of Structural Support Is Needed to Become
Accountable?

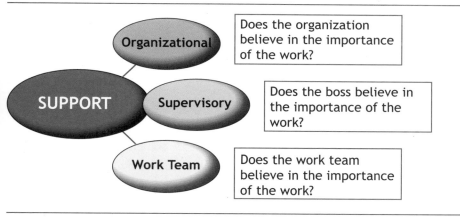

The cultural aspect of support for accountability emerges
from the values and attitudes espoused by the leadership of the
organization. These include attitudes toward learning, respect for
individual differences, tolerance for mistakes made from calculated
risks, and a belief that there is more than one right way to accomplish a goal. Following are some questions you can ask to determine the degree of cultural support at each of the three levels.

- Organizational level
  - Does our organization punish mistakes without fair
    analysis?

- Do people often blame others or circumstances for failed implementations?
- If an individual fails, is he or she given a second chance?

- Supervisory level
  - Does my boss's feedback focus more on "What did we do?" than on "How did we do it?"
  - Does my boss focus more on results or does he or she balance results and processes?
  - Does my boss encourage experimentation?

- Team level
  - Does the team have a can-do attitude?
  - Does the team constantly seek better processes for accomplishing its work?
  - Does the team actively learn from its successes as well as from its mistakes?
  - Do team members readily admit their mistakes?
  - Do team members readily give credit to teammates when it is warranted?

Freedom

There can be no accountability without freedom. Without freedom, there is only organizational responsibility—behaviors that one's salary and job description dictate, and feelings of ownership only to the degree that the individual would like to keep his or her job. There is no accountability if someone else has completely structured and directed the task. The more the structure or system dictates the process and the outcome, the more failure can simply be blamed on the process or on circumstances, and very little real accountability is owned by the employee. The more influence that an individual has over the goals or the process, the more firm is the mental contract that forms the basis of accountability.

Information

Access to essential information is crucial for accountability. In business, the information can be categorized into three major sources: customer focused, supplier or resource focused, and organizational system focused.

Within an organization, managers have both formal and informal communication channels that they use to get the work done. Formal channels travel hierarchical paths, but a manager's informal networks also need to be cultivated to enhance the information flow across boundaries of silos, departments, geography, and functions.

The quality of a manager's decisions is directly proportional to the information sources he or she has access to. For people to feel accountable, they must believe that they have access to enough information. Managers can never wait for perfect information, but they do need to feel that they have or can get access to enough relevant information to come up with an adequate solution in the time allotted.

Resources

All managers live in a resource-constrained world. Yet to feel accountable, managers need access to and control over some of the resources needed to accomplish the tasks of the position. For the typical manager, these resources are capital, personnel, and time.

Although constraints on resources can reduce motivation over time, managers can usually handle the challenge if they feel the shortage is warranted and not arbitrary. For example, across-the-board budget cuts are often difficult to handle, but to meet a specific market challenge or competitor threat, managers often rise to the occasion with innovative approaches.

Goal and Role Clarity

The most crucial aspect of accountability is being extremely clear about *to what* and *to whom* you are accountable. Three major components need to be clarified:

1. To whom are you accountable?
   a. stakeholders
   b. bosses
   c. customers
   d. suppliers
   e. employees
   f. peers
   g. the government
2. What outcomes are you responsible for?
   a. the process
   b. the results
   c. the balance between the two
3. In what areas should I defer or not defer to others?

Managing Polarities

When dealing with issues of goal and role clarity, the components are rarely black or white. People often feel torn between competing commitments. Some of the conflict stems from the myriad priorities that surround the complexities of modern-day business life in a global, financially volatile economy. Managers often report goal confusion and having too many competing priorities. Accountability is difficult in such circumstances.

These types of dilemmas are often referred to as polarities or paradoxes. Each day managers must balance

- short term and long term
- cost, quality, and speed
- low collaboration and high collaboration
- tactical and strategic
- quick fix and long-term solution
- customers' expectations and employees' workloads
- internal versus external focus

The list can feel endless to new managers. In time, experienced leaders manage these tensions constantly and consistently. With this wisdom of experience, accountability can become a core capability for most managers.

Team Accountability

Teams often provide the perfect opportunity to understand accountability. In true teams—those consisting of highly interdependent, differentiated individuals working on complex tasks—group accountability is required if the team is to accomplish its goals. Teammates must trust that fellow members are performing their portion of the team task. Everyone must know the impact and consequences of poor performance on the team's output. Members of true teams feel accountable for the entire body of work of the team—not just their portion of the output—because communication and feedback mechanisms make everyone aware of the progress being made.

Anything less than a true team will struggle with being fully accountable as a group because performance is not always linked through interdependent processes and outcomes. The manager may be held accountable for results, but individual team members are often protected by their respective, seemingly independent processes or goals.

The Leader Accountability Tool

The following tool will help you evaluate a leader in terms of exhibited accountability behaviors and traits. For each area of the model, follow these steps:

1. Make a check mark on the left or right of each statement to indicate whether you definitely agree with it or have some doubt.
2. Review the check marks you have made. If your responses have been predominantly positive (on the right side), then your overall rating should be 6 or higher. If your responses are predominantly on the left side, your rating should be lower. Circle only one of the numbers on the scale from 1 to 10.

Your ratings do not have to be perfect. Use your judgment, given the information you see on the page.

1. Support

The extent to which there is acknowledged support for the importance of our deliverables.

No, Some Doubt   Yes, Definitely

The leader's priorities are highly aligned with the organization's strategy and tactics.

_____   _____

The leader is not hampered by too many top priorities.

_____   _____

The leader's direct supervisor supports our team's priorities.

_____   _____

The leader's team is excited about its results.

_____   _____

| 1 | 2 | 3 | 4 | 5 | 6 | 7 | 8 | 9 | 10 |

Clearly Low   Clearly High

2. Freedom

Overall, the leader has freedom and autonomy to decide how the work should be done.

No, Some
Doubt

Yes,
Definitely

The leader is able to make significant decisions without a high degree of micromanaging by his or her boss.

_____ The leader is able to shape processes for the best results. _____

The leader is able to influence tactics in alignment with strategy.

The leader has the autonomy to direct the work of his or her team or group.

1	2	3	4	5	6	7	8	9	10

Clearly
Low

Clearly
High

3. Information

The leader has access to relevant information in a timely manner.

No, Some
Doubt

Yes,
Definitely

The leader has access to pertinent and reliable customer information.

The leader has access to pertinent and reliable information regarding important resources.

The leader has clear lines of communication throughout the organizational structure.

The leader has effective informal networks to communicate efficiently across organizational boundaries.

1	2	3	4	5	6	7	8	9	10

Clearly
Low

Clearly
High

21

4. Resources

The leader has access to sufficient resources to achieve key priorities.

No, Some   Yes,
Doubt   Definitely

The leader has control of enough capital to achieve
the priorities.

_____   _____

The leader believes he or she has the correct
competencies within the team to create
innovative solutions.

_____   _____

The leader has enough human resources to
accomplish his or her priorities.

_____   _____

The leader believes he or she has adequate time to
accomplish the priorities.

_____   _____

1	2	3	4	5	6	7	8	9	10

Clearly   Clearly
Low   High

5. Goal and Role Clarity

The leader is clear on his or her goals and the role he or she plays in achieving those goals.

No, Some   Yes,
Doubt   Definitely

The leader's team has the right mix of diverse
organizational perspectives.

_____   _____

The leader is clear on who he or she is accountable to.   _____

The leader is clear on the correct balance of ends
versus means (process versus results).

_____   _____

The leader is clear on which tasks need his or her
knowledge or perspective more than other tasks do.   _____

1	2	3	4	5	6	7	8	9	10

Clearly   Clearly
Low   High

Within teams, between teams, and even within and between larger organizational structures such as departments, acknowledged interdependence drives feelings, attitudes, and behaviors of accountability. It basically comes down to knowing the full weight or impact of one's actions on others and truly owning the shared success or failure inherent in those relationships.

In high-performing organizations, collaborative, interdependent structures drive overall effectiveness. These types of organizations often promote accountability as a core value and achieve it. For those organizations that only use the word but don't stand behind it, accountability is often linked to punishment for failure. Managers look for people and processes to blame. These organizations often experience turf wars. People are willing to be accountable only for what they fully control, they want responsibility to be well-defined, and they watch all the short-term metrics because those are the only measures that count.

The Fear Factor

Much of the accountability literature spends a great deal of time talking about the *victim mentality* and describing *victim behavior*. It is helpful to understand and assess victim behavior because it is a clear indicator of fear in the workplace, which, as discussed earlier, is a detriment to accountability. In tremulous times, these may be very real fears of demotion or job loss. More often, small doubts have a way of growing into full-scale paranoia when ambiguity, uncertainty, and a general lack of information are present.

Fear in the workplace is most often centered around feeling threatened by possible repercussions as a result of performance. The relationships of authority are the primary important focal points for fear, and the primary issue is trust—low trust is often a secondary indicator of fear in the workplace. However, in spite of fear in the workplace, many organizations operate successfully. But even these successful organizations could improve if fear were reduced or eliminated.

Organizational cultures often harbor subjects that are not to be openly discussed, such as cross-departmental and regional conflicts or poor financial performance. Problems can occur when there are too many things that people are not supposed to talk about. The health of an organization can commonly be determined by the number of issues that can be discussed in open meetings and the number that require conversations behind closed doors. If people are afraid to speak out about what they know, focus is diverted from productive to nonproductive work, creating a cycle of mistrust. This cycle is reinforced over time, resulting in more fear, gridlock, and other destructive and nonproductive conditions.

Trust can be built through three key behaviors. People are trusted according to whether others see them as

- competent in the task they are required to do
- communicating openly when necessary and keeping things in confidence when asked to do so
- following through on what they say they will do

Trust is built slowly, and when it is lost it takes a long time to rebuild. The best advice is to build it consistently over time.

In organizational life, people are most concerned with:

- negative repercussions or punishment
- a belief that their efforts will not have an effect or change anything
- conflict avoidance
- not wanting to bring attention to themselves

When there is fear, people tend to hide, hold back, and do only what is expected.

Fear is often considered a base emotion that can generate many other secondary emotions, such as aggressiveness, anger, micromanaging, defensiveness, lack of engagement, and victim behavior.

It is important for every manager in an organization to recognize and correct a culture of fear. Here are some steps that leaders can take to turn fear around:

- Listen and observe how employees behave in meetings. Judge the health of meetings by the amount of questions asked as opposed to statements made. Good dialogue suggests that there is a balance of inquiry and advocacy.

- Catch employees doing something right rather than doing something wrong. Provide rich developmental feedback to foster learning and appropriate risk taking.

- Talk to employees and managers who you can count on to be straight with you about their observations on the issue of fear and ask them questions such as: "Are people encouraged to innovate rather than conform?" "Is dissent tolerated in the workplace?" and "What happens when mistakes occur at work? How does leadership respond?"

Most importantly, managers should be encouraged to acknowledge and share their own mistakes and the learning achieved.

Last Words

Accountability has taken on new importance for leaders at all levels. This is mainly because of the increased role that *influencing without authority* plays in performing work under complex business models and environments. Employees claim it is difficult to act with accountability if they don't have the authority to drive decisions. This line of thinking is flawed because it presumes that leadership rests with the individual and not in the collective efforts of teams and groups. CCL has found that there are three keys to strong leadership: *direction, alignment,* and *commitment.* Every individual has ability to create the conditions for leadership and therefore has the opportunity to own responsibility and so become fully accountable.

The ultimate goal of accountability initiatives is to help people take ownership of processes, issues, and decisions in the face of ambiguity and uncertainty. With leadership being a shared responsibility, all members of the organization have accountability for direction, alignment, and a commitment to the collective results of the organization. With ownership comes the responsibility for *doing the right thing* given the best information that can be gathered at the time. If the decisions made were a mistake, then it's leadership's responsibility to determine where the error in judgment was made and to learn from the mistake. In a learning culture, mistakes provide opportunities to clarify assumptions and strategies and to further strengthen performance and innovation. In a culture of fear, however, excuses are made and insights are swept under the rug. In these cultures, leaders are destined to make the same mistakes over and over again.

Suggested Readings

Bossidy, L., & Charan, R. (2002). *Execution: The discipline of getting things done.* New York: Crown Business.

Connors, R., Hickman, C., & Smith, T. (1994). *The Oz principle: Getting results through individual and organizational accountability.* Upper Saddle River, NJ: Prentice Hall.

Goldsmith, W. (2010). *The accountability myth: Why the current leadership models in high-performance sports are failing (badly).* At www.sportscoachingbrain.com/accountabilit/

Lepsinger, R. (2010). *Closing the execution gap: How great leaders and their companies get results.* San Francisco: Pfeiffer.

Miller, J. (1999). *Personal accountability: Powerful and practical ideas for you and your organization.* Denver, CO: Denver Press.

Ryan, K., & Oestreich, D. (1993). *Driving fear out of the workplace: How to overcome the invisible barriers to quality, productivity, and innovation.* San Francisco: Jossey-Bass.

Samuel, M., & Chiche, S. (2004). *The power of personal accountability: Achieve what matters to you.* Katonah, NY: Xephor Press.

Weisbord, M. (1989). *Productive workplaces: Organizing and managing for dignity, meaning, and community.* San Francisco: Jossey-Bass.

Background

The accountability knowledge that CCL has developed is based on five years of extensive study working with major global clients that were seeking assistance in building accountability into their leadership competence models.

The applied research has been based on assessing managers and leaders from these client organizations on a variety of behaviors linked to accountability concepts. These managers and leaders were evaluated using 360-degree assessments and personality instruments designed to define behaviors of effective leaders who demonstrate high levels of accountability.

The participating organizations also went through extensive discovery work to uncover their own definitions of accountability and how it manifests itself in the company culture. Interviews with

senior executives along with staff members from the human resource and organization development departments were also used
to round out the dilemmas and challenges facing organizations
seeking greater accountability in their employees.

In addition to this applied research, studies of innovation by
former CCL scholars Stanley S. Gryskiewicz and Teresa Amabile
were used, with the thinking that innovation and accountability are both intrinsic in nature. Parallel issues were found and a
common process proved useful and therefore was adopted. Two
particularly useful concepts that emerged from this research were
freedom and *encouragement* in creating an environment of accountability.

Background analysis of the literature suggests that the path
to higher accountability begins with engagement followed by
empowerment. Engagement and empowerment literature hold
components of accountability, but accountability literature encap-
sulates all three constructs under one umbrella in an almost developmental path. Employees need to first be engaged, then empowered to make decisions, and finally inspired to take accountability
for doing the right thing.

Key Point Summary

To understand what it takes to foster greater accountability in employees, it must be recognized that this is not *cause-and-effect* work.
Accountability is an intrinsic state of mind for the individual. The
role of managers is to create an environment in which acting with
greater accountability is rewarded and something that is not to be
feared. Too often in organizations, leaders use the word *accountability* as a tool to determine who is to blame. Herein lies the greatest
challenge to building a culture of accountability.

To combat this tendency and create an environment of higher accountability, managers need to provide five key elements. The first is *support*. To be useful, support needs to come from three levels: senior leadership (organizational), the direct supervisor, and the work team. Individuals missing one of these three levels of support will always struggle to be accountable.

The second component is *freedom*. If there is too much direction from the top or from the immediate supervisor, the individual will have no ownership in the process or the results. Although the goal or task needs to be clear, the employee needs freedom to decide how to achieve that goal or task. Without freedom, employees are simply carrying out another person's solution, not one that they own.

Information is the third element. Whether it is from the supply chain, the customer value chain, or the internal information system, managers need to have access to data in order to make sound decisions that they are willing to stand behind.

Resources are the fourth component. Although most managers often find themselves constrained when it comes to resources, to be accountable managers need to believe that they have enough resources to succeed. Arbitrary constraints or simply lacking the necessary combination of capital, people, time, and raw materials can undermine any real feelings of accountability and leave managers with the feeling that the game is stacked against them.

The fifth and most important element is *goal and role clarity*. People need to know to whom they are accountable and for what, and they need to be able to balance accountability for both the process and the results.

In the final analysis, a culture of accountability is one that provides a free flow of information, works to secure viable resources, keeps fear to a minimum, rewards risk taking, and treats mistakes as learning opportunities and not career-ending events. At its core, it is entrepreneurialism. It is taking ownership of all the actions over which individuals have influence given all the available knowledge at their fingertips at that moment, and living with the consequences, good or bad.

Ordering Information

TO GET MORE INFORMATION, TO ORDER OTHER IDEAS INTO ACTION GUIDEBOOKS, OR TO FIND OUT ABOUT BULK-ORDER DISCOUNTS, PLEASE CONTACT US BY PHONE AT 336-545-2810 OR VISIT OUR ONLINE BOOKSTORE AT WWW.CCL.ORG/GUIDEBOOKS.